101 Vegeta

by Carole Eberly

Cover by Kathi Terry

Illustrations by Jerry Wykes

1004 Michigan Ave.

East Lansing, MI 48823

ISBN-0-932296-08-4

TABLE OF CONTENTS

COOKING CHART

(Or what do I do with these now?)

ASPARAGUS-Snap stems—they'll break where tender. Cook whole 8-10 minutes.

BEETS-Cut off stems and roots. Cook 20-30 minutes. The skins will slip off.

BROCCOLI-Clean off leaves and tough stalk ends. Cook 10 minutes.

BRUSSELS SPROUTS-Cut off wilted leaves. Cook 10 minutes.

CABBAGE-Cut into wedges. Cook 8-12 minutes.

CARROTS-Pare. Cook whole 15-20 minutes.

CAULIFLOWER-Pick off leaves. Cook whole 20-25 minutes. Or cut in wedges, cooking 10-15 minutes.

CELERY-Cut off leaves and roots. Cook 8-10 minutes.

CORN-Remove husks and corn silk. Cook 8-10 minutes. For cooking corn kernels, cut kernels from cob. Cook 5-8 minutes.

EGGPLANT-Cut in slices or cubes after paring. Cook 10-15 minutes.

GREEN BEANS-Remove ends and strings. Cook 8-10 minutes.

MUSHROOMS-Cut off bottom of stems. Cook 5-7 minutes.

ONIONS-Peel under cold water (stops the tears). Quarter. Cook 8-10 minutes.

PEAS-Shell. Cook 10-15 minutes.

POTATOES-Pare, if you want. Cook whole 30-40 minutes. Or cook quartered 20-25 minutes. Or cook cubed 10-15 minutes.

SPINACH-Remove roots. Cook 3-5 minutes.

SQUASH (ACORN)-Cut in half. Remove seeds and fiber. Bake cut side down at 350 degrees 40 minutes. Turn right side up and bake another 10-20 minutes.

SQUASH (ZUCCHINI)-Slice. Fry with butter in skillet 5-8 minutes.

SWEET POTATOES-Cook with skins on 30-40 minutes. Peel afterwards, if you want.

TURNIPS-Pare. Slice. Cook 15-20 minutes.

SOME CURES AND OTHER WEIRD THINGS ABOUT VEGETABLES

(I take no responsibility for these things—only reporting what I've discovered.)

—Elizabethan women used carrot leaves in their hair as decorations.

—Hippocrates said onions were good for the sight but bad for the body. (Guess you'd have the best eyesight in the funeral parlor.)

—Onions have been used as cures for dog bites, stomach disorders and earaches. For a chest cold, fried onions (cooled) and plopped on the patient's chest and covered with a cloth was supposed to be just the thing.

—The old onion wart cure went something like this: Cut an onion in half, rub on the wart. Then tie the onion back together and bury it in the ground. The wart disappeared as the onion decayed.

—How cheap are you? Mix onion juice and chicken fat for instant shoe polish.

—Potatoes were once considered suitable only for chickens and pigs.

—Semi-wild tomatoes grow in Peru as high as 50 feet and climb all over bushes and trees.

—More than one hundred million pounds of broccoli are sold each year.

—Drinking tomato juice and eating carrots is supposed to enhance a summer tan.

Appetizers and Snacks

MARINATED BROCCOLI

1 c. vinegar
1 T dill weed
1 T sugar
1 t salt
1 t pepper
1 t garlic salt
1 1/2 c. salad oil
3 bunches broccoli, cut into flowerets

Blend all liquids and spices together. Pour over broccoli in large bowl. Cover and chill 24 hours, turning several times.

SPICY BROCCOLI SPREAD

1/2 lb. chopped broccoli
1 3-oz. pkg. chipped beef
1 16-oz. can tomatoes
2 t chili powder
4 T Worcestershire sauce
4 eggs, beaten
1 lb. cheese spread

Cook broccoli about 5 minutes. Drain and add chipped beef, tomatoes, chili powder and Worcestershire sauce. Add eggs and cook until thick, stirring occasionally. Add cheese to mixture and cook over low heat until cheese melts and mixture thickens. Makes about 4 cups.

CHILLED EGGPLANT SPREAD

1 medium eggplant
1 large onion
3 medium tomatoes
1 clove garlic
1/2 c. salad oil
1 t salt
1 T minced parsley

Bake eggplant for 45 minutes at 375 degrees. Cool. Peel and dice. Peel and finely chop onion, tomatoes and garlic. Mix with the eggplant. Add salad oil, salt and parsley, mixing thoroughly. Serve with crackers.

BUNNY SANDWICH

1 c. grated raw carrots
1/4 c. raisins
1/4 c. chopped nuts
1/4 c. mayonnaise
1 t pickle relish

Mix all ingredients together and spread on bread for sandwiches. Makes enough for 3-5 sandwiches.

FRIED CUCUMBERS

4 medium cucumbers, pared & cut into 1/8-inch slices
1 t salt
1/4 t pepper
3/4 c. dry bread crumbs
1 egg, slightly beaten

Dry cucumbers on paper towels and sprinkle with salt & pepper. Dip into crumbs, then into the egg and back into the crumbs again. Fry in hot (380 degrees) oil until golden. Drain on paper towels. Serves 6-8.

LETTUCE ROLLS

1/4 lb. blue cheese
2 T anchovy paste
Dash paprika
Lettuce

Mix together the blue cheese, anchovy paste and paprika. Chill about 1 hour. Put a small amount on a piece of lettuce and roll up, fastening with a toothpick. Makes a bunch.

ASPARAGUS ROLL-UPS

1/3 c. mayonnaise
Spicy mustard
1/2 lb. thinly sliced ham
1 lb. asparagus spears, cooked and chilled

Make a tangy sauce of mayonnaise and mustard. Spread on a slice of ham. Place an asparagus spear at one end and roll up in the ham. Fasten with toothpicks and chill for 3 hours. Repeat with other slices. Before serving, cut each spear into 3 sections and fasten with a toothpick. Serves 8.

MARINATED BRUSSELS SPROUTS

2 lb. Brussels sprouts
1/3 c. wine vinegar
1 t Dijon mustard
2/3 c. salad oil
1 t dill weed
1 clove garlic, crushed
1/2 t sugar
1/4 t black pepper

Cook Brussels sprouts until just tender—about 10 minutes. Drain and spread out in shallow dish. Mix remaining ingredients well and pour over vegetables. Cover and chill, stirring occasionally, for 24 hours. Drain and serve with tooth picks. Serves 12.

SPINACH DIP

(These following dips go well with almost any raw vegetable hanging around—broccoli, carrots, celery, etc.)

2 c. mayonnaise
4 c. spinach, chopped, cooked & drained
1/2 c. chopped green onion
1/2 c. chopped parsley
1 t salt
1/4 t pepper

Mix all ingredients well. Chill overnight. Makes 3 cups.

CARAWAY DIP

1/2 c. butter
1 8-oz. pkg. cream cheese
1 T finely chopped onion
2 t caraway seed
1 t paprika
1 t dry mustard
1/4 t salt
1/4 t pepper
3/4 c. sour cream

Cream butter and cream cheese. Add remaining ingredients and mix well. Chill about 2 hours. Makes about 2 cups.

DILL WEED DIP

1 c. sour cream
1 c. mayonnaise
1 pkg. onion soup mix
1 T dill weed
1 t Worcestershire sauce
1/2 t Tabasco sauce

Mix all ingredients together well. Let chill about 1 hour. Makes 2 cups.

CURRY DIP

1 c. mayonnaise
2 T tarragon vinegar
1 T curry powder
1 T grated onion
1 T garlic salt
1/4 t pepper

Combine all ingredients well and chill about 2 hours. Makes about 1 cup.

FRENCH FRIED CAULIFLOWER

4 c. cooked cauliflowerets
1 egg, slightly beaten
1 c. dry bread crumbs

Dip cauliflower into egg and roll in crumbs. Fry in hot oil until golden. Drain on paper towels. May be served with shrimp cocktail sauce.

FRIED ONION RINGS

3 c. pancake flour
1/4 c. cream
Beer
Onions
Salt

Slice onions into 1/8-inch thick rings. Mix pancake flour and cream. Add enough beer to make a thick batter. Dip rings into batter and fry in hot oil until golden.

TOMATO CRESCENTS

1 1/2 c. pureed tomatoes
2 t sugar
1/2 t salt
1/4 t onion powder
1/2 t basil leaves
1 pkg. dry tomato soup mix
1/2 c. butter
1 pkg. dry yeast
1 egg white, beaten stiff
2 1/2 - 3 c. flour
Melted butter
Sesame seeds

Heat puree, sugar, salt, onion powder, basil and soup mix to boiling. Add butter and turn off heat. Cool to lukewarm. Add yeast and beat. Stir in beaten egg white. Add flour and beat again. Place in greased bowl, turning once to grease top. Cover with a wet towel and let rise until double. Knead on floured board 3 minutes. Roll out to 1/3-inch thickness. Spread dough with melted butter and sprinkle with sesame seeds. Cut into pie-shaped wedges and roll up into crescents, starting with the wide edge. Place on greased cookie sheets and cover with a wet towel. Let rise until doubled. Bake at 400 degrees for 20 minutes.

(*These* crispy critters are super with spaghetti or other Italian dishes.)

SPOONBREAD

- 2 c. corn
- 1 c. sour cream
- 3 eggs, beaten
- 1/2 c. melted butter
- 1 8 1/2-oz. box corn muffin mix
- 4 oz. grated Swiss cheese

Mix together all ingredients, except cheese. Pour into a 7x11-inch baking dish. Bake at 350 degrees for 35 minutes. Sprinkle cheese over top and bake 10-15 minutes longer.

SWEET POTATO CHIPS

- 2 lb. sweet potatoes, peeled
- 1 T lemon juice
- 4 c. cold water
- Salad oil
- Salt

Cut sweet potatoes into thin slices with potato peeler. Add lemon juice to cold water and soak potato slices in water for 30 minutes. Drain on paper towels. Fry potatoes, a few at a time, in hot oil until dark golden brown. Drain on paper towels. Sprinkle with salt. Makes 4-6 servings.

TOMATO JUICE

1 peck tomatoes, quartered
1/2 bunch celery with leaves, chopped
4 onions, chopped
1 c. sugar
6 t salt
1 t pepper

Simmer tomatoes, celery and onions together until tender. Combine in blender until smooth. Pour back into pot and bring to a boil, adding sugar, salt and pepper. Seal in sterilized jars. Makes about 6 quarts.

JACKSTRAWS

1 medium eggplant
1 c. flour
1 t salt
1 egg, slightly beaten
1 c. milk
1 T salad oil

Cut eggplant in half lengthwise and pare. Slice 1/2-inch thick. Cut slices in 1/2-inch strips. Mix batter with remaining ingredients, beating until smooth. Dip eggplant into batter and fry in hot oil 2-5 minutes, turning once. Sprinkle with salt.

MARINATED MUSHROOMS

3/4 c. olive oil
1/3 c. wine vinegar
1 t salt
1/2 t sugar
1/2 t basil
6 peppercorns
1 clove garlic, quartered
1 bay leaf
1 lb. mushrooms

Stir all ingredients in a saucepan, except mushrooms, and heat to boiling. Simmer, covered, 10 minutes. Stir in mushrooms and cook over medium heat 3-5 minutes. Chill, covered. Drain mushrooms and serve.

SAUSAGE STUFFED MUSHROOMS

1 lb. mushrooms
Salad oil
1/2 lb. bulk spicy pork sausage
1 clove garlic, crushed
1/2 t chopped parsley
1/2 c. fresh bread crumbs
1/3 c. water

Remove stems from caps and chop. Brush caps with oil and place in large baking dish. In a skillet, cook sausage and garlic until done. Drain all but 2 T of drippings. Add parsley, bread crumbs and stems. Fill mushroom caps with mixture. Pour water in baking dish and bake 20 minutes at 350 degrees.

Soups, Salads

and

Preserves

BEST COLE SLAW IN THE WORLD

1 qt. shredded cabbage
1/2 c. shredded green pepper
1/2 c. shredded carrots
2 T grated onion
2 c. cold water
1 1/2 T salt
1 c. sugar
1/2 c. vinegar
1/2 c. water
1 t celery seed
2 c. celery, thinly sliced

Mix cabbage, green pepper, carrots, onion, water and salt in a bowl. Cover and chill 2-4 hours. Heat sugar, vinegar, water and celery seed in saucepan. Bring to a boil. Cool. Drain cabbage well. Mix in celery and pour cooled syrup over mixture. Chill 2-4 hours. Serves 4-6.

COPPER PENNIES

5 c. cooked, sliced carrots
1 medium onion, chopped
1 small green pepper, chopped
1 c. sugar
1/2 c. salad oil
1 can tomato soup
1 t mustard
1 t salt
1/4 t pepper
1/4 c. vinegar
1 t Worcestershire sauce

Mix together carrots, onion and green pepper. Heat remaining ingredients in saucepan until sugar melts and everything is well-blended. Pour over carrot mixture and chill overnight. Serves 4-6.

TOMATO BUTTER

(An old Shaker recipe)

Peel seven pounds of ripe tomatoes. Add three pounds light brown sugar, half a pint of vinegar and half an ounce of cinnamon. Boil slowly 5-6 hours. Bottle. This can be added to almost any soup or sauce.

GREEN BEAN SALAD

2 c. green beans, cooked
2 T cream
2 t tarragon vinegar
4 T prepared mustard
2 T sugar
2 T chopped green onions
Dash salt
Dash pepper

Thoroughly chill green beans. Combine other ingredients and pour over green beans before serving.

WILTED LETTUCE

1 head lettuce, shredded
1/4 t salt
3 slices bacon
1 small onion, diced
1/2 c. vinegar
1 T sugar
1 hard boiled egg, sliced

Cut lettuce into 1-inch strips and put in serving dish. Sprinkle with salt and let stand 10 minutes. Fry bacon until crisp. Remove and break into small pieces. Cook onion in bacon fat until tender. Add vinegar and sugar. When hot, pour over lettuce and mix well. Sprinkle with bacon and garnish with egg slices. Serves 6-8.

CAULIFLOWER SALAD

1 head cauliflower
1 c. mayonnaise
1 T Dijon mustard
1 T lemon juice
1 T sugar
1/4 c. black olives, pitted & sliced

Cut cauliflower into bite-size pieces. Cover with boiling water and let stand until cool. Drain. Mix mayonnaise, mustard, lemon juice and sugar together. Add to cauliflower, mixing well. Garnish with olives. Chill 2-4 hours.

ZUCCHINI SALAD

(Here's one way to get rid of that monster zucchini sitting in your refrigerator.)

10 lb. zucchini, sliced thin
4 lb. tomatoes, quartered
4 lb. onions, sliced
1 gal. salad oil
1 1/2 qt. vinegar
4 T prepared mustard
4 T salt
1 T pepper
2 T oregano

Mix all ingredients in a large crock. Let stand for seven days, turning daily. Serves millions.

SPINACH AND MUSHROOM SALAD

4 c. spinach, torn into bite-size pieces
2 c. sliced mushrooms
1 medium onion, sliced
1/2 c. blue cheese, crumbled
1 clove garlic, crushed
1 t salt
1/2 t parsley, shopped
6 T salad oil
2 T white vinegar

In a salad bowl, mix together spinach, mushrooms and onion. In a small jar shake remaining ingredients. Pour over vegetables. Serves 4.

BEET-HORSERADISH MOLDED SALAD

2 c. beets
3 T vinegar
3-oz. pkg. lemon gelatin
1/2 t salt
3/4 c. celery, chopped
2 T horseradish
1 T onion, finely chopped

Cook beets. Reserve enough liquid to make 1 1/2 cups, adding more water if necessary. Heat liquid and vinegar. Add gelatin and stir until dissolved. Add salt. Chill until mixture thickens to consistency of egg whites. Fold in celery, horseradish, onion and beets cut into small pieces. Chill in an 8 x 8-inch pan. Serves 8.

RUSSIAN POTATO SALAD

1/2 c. salad oil
1/4 c. vinegar
1 T Dijon mustard
1 clove garlic, minced
1 T chopped parsley
1 T chopped chives
1/4 t pepper
3 c. mushrooms, sliced
4 c. romaine lettuce, torn
3 medium potatoes, cooked, peeled, diced & chilled
2 c. beets, cooked, sliced & chilled
2 hard-boiled eggs, sliced

Mix together salad oil, vinegar, mustard, garlic, parsley, chives and pepper. Pour over mushrooms and chill 2 hours. Place lettuce in salad bowl and cover with potatoes and beets. Spoon mushrooms on top with dressing. Garnish with egg slices. Serves 6-8.

CAESAR SALAD

1 large head romaine lettuce
1/3 c. olive oil
2 cloves garlic
1 lemon
1 egg
Salt
1/4 t Worcestershire sauce
Pepper
6 T grated Parmesan cheese
1 c. croutons

Wash and thoroughly dry lettuce leaves. Place in salad bowl. Pour salad oil into blender. Add garlic cloves, juice of one lemon, egg, dash of salt, Worcestershire sauce and pepper; blend well. Pour over lettuce leaves. Sprinkle with cheese and mix thoroughly. Sprinkle croutons on top. Serves 4-6.

MARINATED LIMA BEANS

- 4 c. lima beans, cooked
- 4 T salad oil
- 1 c. sour cream
- 2 T tarragon vinegar
- 1 t salt
- 2 T parsley, chopped
- 1 t sugar

Drain lima beans. Combine the remaining ingredients and pour over beans. Chill 2-4 hours. Serve on beds of lettuce. Serves 8.

PICKLED CAULIFLOWER

- 1 lg. head cauliflower
- 1/3 c. white wine vinegar
- 2 cloves
- 1/2 cinnamon stick
- 2 t sugar
- 1/2 t salt
- 1/4 t pepper

Break cauliflower into flowerets and cook until tender. Drain. Stir in remaining ingredients and chill, covered. Serves 4.

CUCUMBER SOUP

4 cucumbers, peeled & seeded
1 T salt
1 c. yogurt
3 ice cubes
1 T lemon juice
1/4 c. water
1 T tarragon
Dash pepper
1/4 t chives

Dice cucumbers and sprinkle with salt. Let stand 1/2 hour. Drain. Put all ingredients in blender and mix well. Strain and chill. Serves 4.

CREAM OF MUSHROOM SOUP

1 lb. mushrooms, cut up
4 c. water
2 T butter
1 T flour
1 c. cream
Salt & pepper

Bring mushrooms to a boil in water. Lower heat and simmer 1 hour. Strain liquid into double boiler. Heat butter and flour, adding 1/4 c. liquid and stirring constantly until smooth. Add to liquid in double boiler. Cook until hot. Five minutes before serving, add cream and salt and pepper to taste. Serves 6.

FRENCH ONION SOUP

6 large onions, sliced
3 T butter
6 c. beef stock
1 t Worcestershire sauce
1 t sherry
Toast slices
Romano cheese

Brown onions in butter until golden. Add stock, Worcestershire sauce and sherry. Simmer 25 minutes. Pour into serving dishes and place a toast slice over each. Pile on the Romano cheese. Place under broiler until cheese melts slightly. Serves 6.

SPLIT PEA SOUP

2 c. split peas
4 c. water
1 t salt
1 T butter
1 medium onion, chopped
1 medium carrot, chopped
1 bay leaf
Pinch thyme
1 c. diced, cooked ham
Croutons

Soak peas in water to cover about 1 hour. Drain and bring to a boil with the 4 c. water and salt. In saucepan, saute onion, carrot, bay leaf and thyme. Add to peas and continue cooking about 1 hour or until peas are soft. Add more water, if too thick. Add ham and continue simmering 1/2 hour. Sprinkle with croutons. Serves 6.

GAZPACHO

4 medium tomatoes, peeled
2 cucumbers, peeled & sliced
1/2 green pepper, seeded & sliced
1 clove garlic, minced
2 T olive oil
3 T vinegar
6 slices bread, cubed
4 ice cubes
3 1/2 c. water
1 1/2 t pepper

Combine all ingredients in blender until smooth. Chill. Soup should be thick, but if too thick, add a little ice water. Garnish with minced green pepper. Serves 6-8.

PUMPKIN BISQUE

2 T butter
1/2 c. onion, chopped
4 c. mashed pumpkin
1 1/2 c. chicken broth
2 c. evaporated milk
1 T lemon juice
2 T sugar
2 t salt
1/2 t cinnamon
Dash pepper

Saute onion in butter until tender. Stir in remaining ingredients and cook, stirring occasionally, until soup boils. Lower heat and simmer 10 minutes. Serves 6.

BORSCHT

1 gal. beef stock
1 lb. onions
Butter
1 lb. cabbage, shredded
4 c. beets, cooked & shredded
1/2 c. tomato paster
3 c. tomatoes, peeled
2 cloves garlic, crushed
1 c. beet juice
1 T lemon juice
1 T sugar
1 T vinegar
1 T salt
Sour cream

Heat beef stock in large pot. Saute onions in butter until tender. Add to the beef stock with cabbage, beets, tomato paste, tomatoes and garlic. Let boil slowly for 15-20 minutes. Add beet juice, lemon juice, sugar, vinegar and salt. Let simmer 15 minutes. Serve as is, or strained, hot or cold with sour cream. Serves 10.

CABBAGE SOUP

1/2 medium head cabbage, shredded
6 c. chicken stock
1 large onion, chopped
1 T salt
1 T sugar
4 peppercorns
1 bay leaf
3 T Worcestershire sauce
1 lb. ground beef
2 c. tomato paste

Combine all ingredients, except ground beef and tomato paste. Bring to a boil and simmer 1 hour. Cook ground beef until done. Drain and add to soup with tomato paste. Simmer 15 more minutes. Serves 6.

HEARTY WINTER SOUP

2 lb. beef shank
Oil
2 qt. water
1 medium onion, chopped
1 T salt
1/4 t pepper
1 clove garlic, minced
1 T parsley, chopped
3 stalks celery, sliced
2 t Worcestershire sauce
2 bay leaves
2 c. cabbage, shredded
2 c. carrots, sliced
2 c. potatoes, diced
2 c. tomatoes
1/2 t oregano

Cut meat from bones and brown in hot oil. Add meat and bones to water. Add onion, salt, pepper, garlic and parsley. Bring to a boil, lower heat, cover and simmer 2 hours. Add remaining ingredients and simmer 1 hour. Remove bones and serve. Serves 8-10.

POTATO-TURNIP SOUP

3 medium potatoes
3 small turnips
2 medium onions
4 carrots
1 stalk celery
2 t chopped parsley
1 T salt
5 peppercorns
Water
2 c. milk
3 T butter
1/2 t allspice

Chop vegetables into fairly large chunks. Put in pot with enough water to cover about 3/4 of the vegetables. Add parsley, salt and peppercorns. Bring to a boil, then simmer until vegetables are soft, about 1 hour. Pour into blender and mix well. Pour back into pot and add milk, butter and allspice. Simmer until hot. Serves 6-8.

Side Dishes

HARVARD BEETS

- 1/3 c. sugar
- 2 T flour
- 1/4 c. beet liquid
- 1/2 c. vinegar
- 1/2 t salt
- 2 T butter
- 2 c. beets, cooked & sliced

Mix sugar and flour in saucepan. Add beet liquid and vinegar. Cook over medium heat until thick, stirring occasionally. Add salt, butter and beets. Coat beets thoroughly. Serves 4.

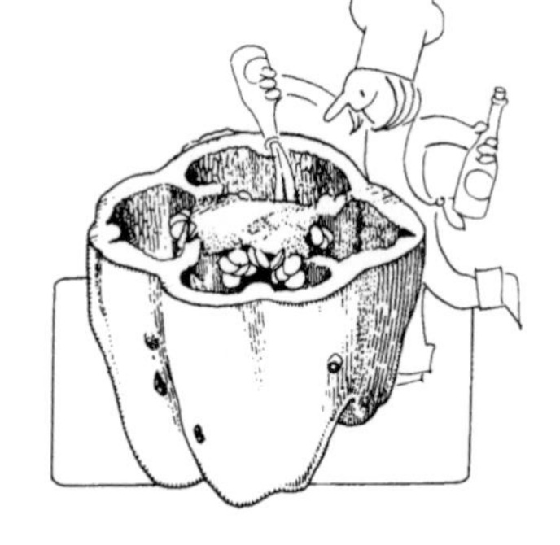

BROWN BUTTERED BRUSSELS SPROUTS

1 qt. Brussels sprouts
1 1/2 c. water
3 T butter
1 T lemon juice
Almonds

Cook Brussels sprouts in boiling water until tender, about 10-15 minutes. Drain. In skillet heat butter until light brown. Stir in lemon juice. Pour over Brussels sprouts, mixing well. Sprinkle with almonds. Serves 6.

ASPARAGUS ALMONDINE

(So easy, so good!)

2 lb. asparagus
1/4 lb. butter
1/4 c. silvered almonds
Juice of 1/2 lemon

Cook asparagus just until tender, about 10 minutes. In a skillet, fry almonds in butter until golden brown. Add lemon juice. Place asparagus on serving dish and pour sauce on top. Serves 6.

ITALIAN CARROTS & PEAS

1 lb. carrots, cooked & sliced
2 c. peas, cooked
1 c. salad oil
1/4 c. vinegar
1 t salt
1/4 t pepper
1/4 t sugar
1/4 t cayenne
1/4 t dry mustard
1 clove garlic, minced
1 t parsley, chopped
Dash Tabasco sauce

Marinate vegetables in remaining ingredients 2 hours before serving. May be served hot or cold. Serves 6.

PEAS IN SOUR CREAM

2 c. peas
1/4 c. water
1 t salt
1/2 t tarragon
Dash pepper
1/2 c. sour cream
1/2 c. mayonnaise
1 T lemon juice

Cook peas in water, salt, tarragon and pepper about 10 minutes. Heat sour cream, mayonnaise and lemon juice in double boiler, stirring frequently. Add vegetables and heat. Serves 8.

MINTED PEAS

2 T vinegar
1/3 c. salad oil
1/2 t paprika
1/4 t salt
1 t mint leaves, minced
4 c. peas, cooked & chilled

Mix all ingredients together, except peas. Pour over peas and stir well. Chill 2 hours. Serves 6-8.

OVEN FRIED POTATOES

8 large unpeeled potatoes,
each cut in 8 wedges
1/2 c. salad oil
1 t salt
1/2 t garlic powder
1/2 t paprika
2 T grated Parmesan cheese

Place potato wedges, peel side down, in shallow baking dishes. Mix remaining ingredients together and brush over potatoes. Bake at 375 degrees for about 45 minutes, so until golden, brushing occasionally with oil mixture. Serves 8.

POTATO BALLS

2 c. mashed potatoes
2 T butter
1 t salt
1 t sugar
2 egg yolks
2 egg whites, beaten
Butter

Mix together all ingredients, except butter. Form into 1-inch balls. Brush with melted butter. Bake at 350 degrees about 30 minutes. Serves 4.

GREEN RICE

4 c. cooked rice
3 eggs, beaten
1 1/4 c. milk
1/2 c. butter
1/2 c. grated cheddar cheese
3/4 T onion, grated
1/2 c. parsley, chopped
1 c. spinach, minced
1 1/2 t Worcestershire sauce
2 t salt

Mix all ingredients together well. Pour into greased casserole. Bake at 325 degrees for about 45 minutes. Serves 8.

SPINACH SOUFFLE

4 c. spinach, cooked & chopped
1 onion, minced
1 c. mushrooms
4 T butter
1 can cream of mushroom soup
2 eggs, beaten
1/4 c. Parmesan cheese

Saute onion and mushrooms in butter. Add cooked spinach. Remove from heat and add soup and eggs. Pour into greased casserole. Sprinkle with Parmesan cheese. Bake at 350 degrees for 30 minutes. Serves 4-6.

SPINACH CASSEROLE

6 c. spinach, cooked & chopped
1 pkg. onion soup mix
2 c. sour cream
3 T butter
3/4 c. crushed dry stuffing

Mix sour cream and onion soup mix with spinach. Spread in greased casserole. Sprinkle stuffing on top. Dot with butter. Bake at 400 degrees for 25 minutes. Serves 8-10.

BAKED SWEET POTATOES & APPLES

1 lb. sweet potatoes
2 apples, peeled & sliced
1/4 c. brown sugar
1 t cinnamon
1 t salt
1/4 c. butter
1/2 c. water

Partially cook potatoes. Peel and slice in 1/2-inch pieces. Place a layer of potatoes on bottom of greased casserole. Top with a layer of apples. Add half the sugar, cinnamon, salt and butter. Repeat with remaining ingredients. Pour water over mixture. Cover and bake at 375 degrees for 45 minutes. Serves 4.

STEWED TOMATOES

4 slices bacon
4 c. tomatoes, peeled
1 small green pepper, grated
1 small onion, grated
1/2 t salt
6 drops Tabasco sauce
1/2 c. bread crumbs

Fry bacon until crisp. Crumble in pan. Brown green pepper and onion with fried bacon. Add tomatoes, salt and tobasco; cook 5 minutes. Add bread crumbs. Serves 6-8.

TURNIP CASSEROLE

2 c. turnips, cooked & mashed
1 T sugar
1 t salt
Dash pepper
2 eggs, beaten
1 c. dry bread crumbs
3 T butter

Combine turnips, sugar, salt, pepper and eggs. Stir in 1/2 bread crumbs. Pour into greased casserole. Top with remaining bread crumbs and dot with butter. Serves 4-6.

STIR-FRIED ASPARAGUS

2 lb. asparagus
1 T cornstarch
1/2 c. chicken broth
2 T sherry
1 T soy sauce
1/2 t sugar
1/4 t dry mustard
3 T salad oil
1 clove garlic, crushed

Cut asparagus into 1-inch diagonal slices. In a bowl, mix cornstarch and broth. Stir in sherry, soy sauce, sugar and dry mustard. Heat oil in skillet and quickly cook asparagus, stirring all the while, about 3-4 minutes. Sprinkle with salt and add garlic to skillet. Stir in cornstarch mixture and continue stirring until mixture thickens and coats asparagus. Serves 6.

ASPARAGUS CASSEROLE

3 c. asparagus, cooked
2 T butter, melted
2 T flour
2 c. milk
1/2 c. grated cheddar cheese
1/4 t salt
Dash pepper
3/4 c. dry bread crumbs
2 T butter

Place asparagus in casserole. In a saucepan, make a paste of butter and flour. Gradually add milk, stirring constantly until thickened. Add cheese, salt and pepper. Pour over asparagus. Sprinkle with bread crumbs and dot with butter. Bake at 325 degrees for 30 minutes. Serves 6-8.

CURRIED CAULIFLOWER

1 lg. head cauliflower
1 can cream of mushroom soup
4 oz. grated cheddar cheese
1/3 c. mayonnaise
1 t curry
1/2 c. buttered dry bread crumbs

Break cauliflower into flowerets and cook until tender. Drain. Heat next four ingredients until cheese melts. Add to cauliflower and pour into greased casserole. Top with buttered crumbs. Bake at 350 degrees about 30 minutes. Serves 6.

BRUSSELS SPROUTS IN CHEESE SAUCE

1 qt. Brussels sprouts
1 1/2 c. water
2 T butter
2 T flour
2 c. milk
1/3 c. grated Swiss cheese
1/8 t nutmeg

Cook Brussels sprouts in water until tender, about 10-15 minutes. In a saucepan, make a paste of butter and flour. Slowly add milk, stirring constantly until thickened. Add Swiss cheese and nutmeg. Pour over Brussels sprouts. Serves 6.

FRIED CABBAGE

(Sort of like Wilted lettuce.)

- 2 lb. cabbage, shredded
- 3 strips bacon
- 1/4 c. vinegar
- 1 t sugar
- 1 t salt
- 1/4 t pepper

Fry bacon until crisp and break into pieces. Add cabbage and saute, stirring constantly. Add remaining ingredients, mixing well. Serves 6.

CELERY & ALMOND CASSEROLE

- 5 c. chopped celery
- 1/2 slivered almonds
- 1 c. mushrooms, chopped
- 2 cans cream of chicken soup
- 1/2 c. grated cheddar cheese
- 1 c. dry bread crumbs
- Paprika

Mix the celery, almonds and mushrooms in a greased casserole dish. Pour soup over and mix well. Sprinkle with grated cheese and bread crumbs. Sprinkle with a dash of paprika. Cover and bake at 375 degrees for 25 minutes. Remove cover and let brown about 20 minutes.

CORN & TOMATO CASSEROLE

2 1/2 c. tomatoes, peeled
2 1/2 c. cooked corn
1 small green pepper, chopped
1/2 c. dry bread crumbs
2 T melted butter
1 t onion salt
Dash pepper
1 t sugar
1/2 c. grated cheddar cheese
Butter

Mix together tomatoes, corn, green pepper, bread crumbs and melted butter. Stir in seasonings. Place in greased casserole and sprinkle with cheese; dot with butter. Bake at 350 degrees for 1 hour. Serves 8.

CREOLE STYLE GREEN BEANS

6 slices bacon
1/2 c. onion, chopped
1/2 c. green pepper, chopped
2 T flour
2 T sugar
2 t Worcestershire sauce
1/2 t salt
Dash pepper
1/8 t dry mustard
2 c. tomatoes, peeled
3 c. green beans, cooked

Fry bacon until crisp and break into small pieces. Remove from skillet and add onion and green pepper, cooking until tender. Drain all but 3 T bacon drippings from pan. Blend in flour, sugar, Worcestershire sauce, salt, pepper and mustard. Add tomatoes, stirring over medium heat until thickened. Add green beans and heat. Top with crumbled bacon. Serves 8.

BARBECUED LIMA BEANS

4 c. lima beans, cooked
1/2 lb. bacon
1 small onion, sliced
1/2 c. brown sugar
1 1/2 c. lima bean water
2 T prepared mustard
2 t Worcestershire sauce
1 t oregano
1 c. tomato sauce
1/3 c. vinegar

Fry half the bacon until crisp. Remove. Saute onion in bacon fat. Add brown sugar, bean water, mustard, Worcestershire sauce, oregano, tomato sauce and vinegar. Simmer 15 minutes. Alternate beans and sauce in casserole. Cover with remaining bacon strips. Bake at 400 degrees for 30 minutes. Serves 6-8.

SUCCOTASH

- 2 c. corn, cooked
- 2 c. lima beans, cooked
- 4 T pimento, chopped
- 2 T butter
- 1 t salt
- 1/8 t pepper

Mix all ingredients together and heat thoroughly. Serves 6.

CHEESE ONIONS

- 6 medium onions, peeled
- 1 t salt
- 2 T butter
- 2 T water
- 1 c. grated cheddar cheese
- 2 T parsley, chopped

Cut onions into 1/2-inch slices. Place in greased casserole. Add salt, butter and water. Cover and bake 1 hour at 350 degrees. Remove cover and sprinkle with cheese. Re-cover and return to oven to melt cheese. Sprinkle with parsley. Serves 4.

BRAISED CELERY

2 large onions, sliced
4 c. celery, sliced
4 T butter
1 T cornstarch
2 c. chicken broth
Salt & pepper

Place onions in greased baking dish. Brown celery in butter. Mix cornstarch with a little water, then add to chicken stock. Pour in with celery and cook until thickened, about 5 minutes. Season with salt and pepper. Pour over onions and bake at 325 degrees for 1 hour. Serves 6.

CARROT SOUFFLE

3 T butter
3 T flour
1/4 t salt
1/2 t sugar
1 c. milk
3 eggs, separated
2 c. cooked carrots, mashed

Mix together over medium heat butter, flour, salt and sugar. Slowly add milk, stirring constantly, until thick. Beat egg yolks. Add a little of the white sauce to the yolks. Slowly mix in white sauce with yolks. Stir in carrots and cool. Beat egg whites until stiff. Fold into mixture. Pour into greased casserole. Place in pan of hot water and bake at 350 degrees 45-50 minutes. Serves 6.

CORN & BACON PUDDING

3 c. corn, cooked
3 eggs
1/4 c. cream
1 t salt
Dash pepper
3 T minced onion
1/4 t baking powder
1/2 c. grated cheddar cheese
3 slices bacon, cut in 1" pieces

Mix all ingredients together, except cheese and bacon. Pour into a greased casserole. Cover with cheese and bacon. Bake at 350 degrees 40-45 minutes. Serves 6.

GREEN BEAN CASSEROLE

(A favorite old stand-by)

3 c. green beans, cooked
3/4 c. milk
1 T minced pimento
1 can cream of mushroom soup
1 can French fried onion rings

Mix together beans, milk, pimento, soup and 1/2 can onion rings. Pour into greased casserole. Bake at 350 degrees for 20 minutes. Garnish with rest of onions and bake 5 minutes longer. Serves 6.

BROCCOLI ROMANO

- 2 1/2 lb. broccoli, cooked
- Butter
- Salt & pepper
- 3/4 c. grated Romano cheese

Season broccoli with butter, salt and pepper. Sprinkle with Romano cheese. Serves 6-8. *(Simple, huh?)*

ITALIAN EGGPLANT CASSEROLE

- 1 large eggplant
- 3 eggs, beaten
- 1 c. dry bread crumbs
- Salad oil
- 3/4 c. Parmesan cheese
- 2 t oregano
- 1/2 lb. Mozzarella cheese, sliced
- 3 c. tomato sauce

Pare eggplant and slice into 1/4-inch pieces. Dip each into eggs and then coat with bread crumbs. Fry in hot oil until golden. Layer eggplant in casserole with Parmesan cheese, oregano and Mozzarella cheese. Top with tomato sauce. Bake at 350 degrees for 30 minutes.

Main Dishes

SAUSAGE, SAUERKRAUT & POTATO CASSEROLE

10-oz. pkg. Smokey links
2 c. sauerkraut
3 medium potatoes, chopped
2 eggs, beaten
1 t salt
1/2 t pepper
1/2 c. grated cheddar cheese

Cut links into 1-inch pieces. Place half the sauerkraut in greased casserole. Add a layer of meat. Mix together potatoes, eggs, salt and pepper. Place a layer of potato mixture over meat. Repeat layers. Cover and bake 1 hour. Remove cover and sprinkle cheese on top. Return casserole to oven and bake 15 minutes longer. Serves 4.

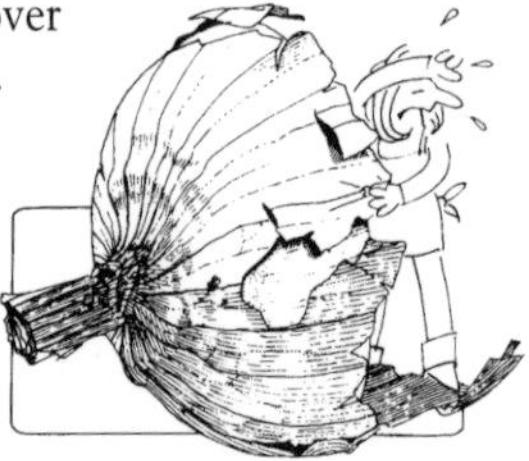

GREEN PEPPER STEAK

1 lb. flank steak
4 T soy sauce
2 T sherry
1 T sugar
1 t cornstarch
1 large green pepper
4 stalks celery
1 small onion
1 medium tomato
Salad oil

Cut steak into strips 1/4-inch wide. Marinate in mixture of soy sauce, sherry, sugar and cornstarch. Slice green pepper into strips and cut celery diagonally. Slice onion into rings and cube the tomato. Saute steak in small amount of oil until light pink. Add green pepper, celery and onion and saute until tender. Just before serving add the tomato. Serve over rice. Serves 4.

SWEET POTATO BAKE

2 medium sweet potatoes
1 lb. pork sausage, sliced
4 apples
2 t sugar
1/4 t cinnamon

Peel and slice sweet potatoes in bottom of baking dish. Add layer of sliced sausage. Peel and slice apples over top, sprinkle with sugar and cinnamon. Cover and bake 1 hour at 375 degrees. Serves 4.

SPICY PEPPER SKILLET

1/4 c. salad oil
3 lg. onions, sliced
6 lg. green peppers, sliced
1 c. sliced mushrooms
1 c. seasoned tomato sauce
1 lb. cooked Italian sausage, sliced
2 t seasoned salt
2 t garlic salt
2 t oregano
2 t basil

Saute onions in salad oil. Add remaining ingredients and simmer, covered, 20-30 minutes. Serves 6.

STUFFED CUCUMBERS

3 medium cucumbers
1/2 c. chicken, cooked & chopped
1 c. shrimp, cooked & chopped
1 stalk celery, chopped
1 T onion, minced
1/2 c. mayonnaise
2 T lemon juice
2 T tomato sauce
1 T chili sauce
Salt & pepper

Peel cucumbers and cut in half lengthwise. Scoop out seeds. Mix together chicken, shrimp, celery and onion. Combine mayonnaise, lemon juice, tomato sauce and chili sauce for dressing. Season with salt and pepper. Mix dressing with chicken mixture. Spoon into cucumbers. Serves 6.

VEGETABLE-CHEESE BAKE

1 T salad oil
1 large onion, chopped
1 large pepper, chopped
1 small eggplant, pared & cut into 1-inch cubes
1/2 lb. mushrooms, sliced
1 large tomato, chopped
1 t salt
1/2 t basil
1 c. stuffing mix
2 c. grated Swiss cheese

Saute onion and green pepper in oil 3 minutes. Add eggplant and mushrooms. Saute 3 minutes, stirring constantly. Add tomato, salt and basil, cooking 1 minute. Pour stuffing mix over bottom of greased large casserole dish. Layer half vegetable mixture and 1 cup of cheese over stuffing. Top with remaining vegetables. Bake, covered, at 350 degrees for 30 minutes. Sprinkle with remaining cheese and bake, uncovered, 10 minutes. Serves 4-6.

MUSHROOM STRATA

1 lb. mushrooms, sliced
2 T butter
1/2 c. mayonnaise
1 t salt
1/4 t pepper
1/2 c. onions, chopped
1/2 c. celery, chopped
1/2 c. green pepper, chopped
2 eggs, beaten
1 1/2 c. milk
1 can cream of mushroom soup
8 slices bread
Butter

Butter bread and cut into cubes. Put 3 slices of the bread into bottom of greased casserole. Saute mushrooms in butter. Mix mushrooms, onions, celery and green pepper together with mayonnaise, salt and pepper. Put in casserole over bread cubes. Top with 3 more slices cubed bread. Two hours before baking, mix eggs and milk together and pour over vegetables. Chill at least 2 hours. Before baking, spoon on soup and top with last 2 slices of bread. Bake at 300 degrees for 1 1/2 hours. Serves 6-8.

CHARLES NICHOLSON'S FAMOUS SPAGHETTI

(A disclaimer—I take no responsibility for the following method Mr. Nicholson uses in his preparation. However, the results are fantastic!)

MEAT BALLS

- 2-3 pre-teen children
- 1 large bag potato chips
- 6 pack of Coke
- 3 lb. ground round
- 1-2 eggs
- 1 c. cracker or bread crumbs
- 3/4 c. diced onion
- Italian seasoning

Prepare 2-3 pre-teen children for meat balls by washing thoroughly and stuffing with chips and Coke. Take 1/2 to 1/3 of stuffed children and use to mix thoroughly the ground round, eggs, crumbs, onions and seasoning. Instruct children to begin making meat balls from mixture. (I make a couple of samples to insure uniform size—smaller than a ping-pong ball, larger than a grape.) While meat balls are being "sized," take remaining children to begin to brown sized meat balls in a skillet.

NOW THE SAUCE

- 1 liter Rose wine
- 1/2 clove garlic
- 1 c. diced onion, sauteed
- 1-2 shakes parsley flakes
- Italian seasoning
- 1/4 c. sugar
- 1/4 t dried red peppers
- Some cans of tomato sauce
- 2 6-oz. cans tomato paste
- 1 6 1/2-oz. can mushrooms

Take chilled Rose wine, uncork and allow to breathe. Decant into goblet of your choice or clean coffee cup. Sip while observing meat ball process. (One liter is usually sufficient for meat balls.)

Place browned meat balls into large 4 1/2-qt. kettle along with onions and garlic. Add seasonings, tomato paste and enough cans of tomato sauce to bring level to half-way mark. Add enough water to increase level to 2/3 mark. Store remaining cans of sauce until next time.

Simmer sauce for 2 hours or until guests arrive. Mix in mushrooms 10 minutes before serving. Serves 4-6 people, depending on people.

STUFFED SQUASH

4 acorn squash
1 lb. ground beef
1 c. onion, chopped
1 c. tomato sauce
1 t honey
1/2 t cinnamon
Dash nutmeg
1/8 t pepper
1/2 c. water
1/2 c. raisins
1 1/2 c. cooked rice
1 c. shredded Swiss cheese

Cut squash in half and scoop out seeds and fiber. Place cut side down on a greased roasting pan and bake 40 minutes at 375 degrees. Cook beef and onion together in a skillet. Drain well. Stir in tomato sauce, honey, cinnamon, nutmeg, pepper, water and raisins. Simmer 5 minutes, stirring occasionally. Remove from heat and stir in rice and cheese. Remove squash from oven and turn right side up. Fill with meat mixture. Bake 20-25 minutes or until squash is tender. Serves 8.

SPANISH CHICKEN & RICE

3 lb. chicken, cut up
Salt & pepper
3/4 c. salad oil
2 c. raw rice
1 medium onion, chopped
1 green pepper, chopped
1 c. chicken stock
2 c. tomatoes
1 t salt
1/2 t paprika

Season chicken with salt and pepper. Brown chicken in salad oil. Remove from pan and pour off about 1/2 cup oil. Brown rice, onion and green pepper in remaining oil. Add remaining ingredients, stirring well. Place chicken on top of rice. Cover and simmer. Cook about 25 minutes, or until rice is tender and liquid absorbed. Serves 4-6.

ONION PIE

3 c. onions, sliced thin
3 T butter
1 1/2 c. yogurt
1/2 c. evaporated milk
2 eggs, beaten
1 1/2 t salt
1/4 t pepper
1/8 t nutmeg
1/8 t ginger
9-inch baked pie shell

Saute onions in butter until golden. Mix in other ingredients, except pie shell. *(You knew that anyway, though, didn't you?)* Pour into pie shell and bake at 450 degrees for 10 minutes. Lower heat to 350 degrees and bake another 45 minutes, or until knife blade inserted in center comes out clean. Serves 6.

SQUASH LASAGNA

- 4 lg. zucchini
- 2 T salad oil
- 2 cloves garlic, minced
- 1/2 c. onion, chopped
- 1/2 lb. ground beef
- 2 c. tomatoes
- 6-oz. can tomato paste
- 1/2 c. mushrooms, sliced
- 3/4 c. red wine
- 1 1/2 t oregano
- 1/4 t thyme
- 1 t basil
- Salt & pepper
- 8 oz. Mozzarella cheese, sliced
- 1 c. grated Parmesan cheese

Cut zucchini into 1/4-inch strips. Saute zucchini, onion and garlic in oil until vegetables are tender, but firm. Remove and add meat to brown. When crumbly, add tomatoes, tomato paste, mushrooms, wine, herbs and salt and pepper to taste. Simmer, uncovered, 1 1/2 hours. Place half zucchini strips in greased baking dish. Top with half the Mozzarella cheese. Add half meat sauce. Repeat layers. Top with Parmesan cheese. Bake at 350 degrees for 30 minutes. Serves 6.

CURRIED CHICKEN & BROCCOLI

4 chicken breasts, cooked & sliced
1 large bunch broccoli
1 can cream of chicken soup
2/3 c. mayonnaise
1/3 c. cream
1/2 c. grated mild cheese
1 t lemon juice
1/2 t curry powder
1 c. dry bread crumbs
2 T butter

Cook broccoli just until tender. Place in casserole. Slice chicken and place on top. Combine soup, mayonnaise, cream, cheese, lemon juice and curry. Pour over chicken and sprinkle with bread crumbs. Dot with butter. Bake at 350 degrees for 30 minutes. Serves 4-6.

SQUASH PIE

1 1/2 c. squash, cooked & mashed
3/4 c. sugar
1 t ginger
1 t cinnamon
1/2 t nutmeg
1/2 t salt
1/4 t cloves
3 eggs
1 c. milk
2 c. evaporated milk
1 9-inch unbaked pie shell

Mix together squash, sugar, spices and salt. Beat in eggs, milk and evaporated milk. Pour into pie shell and bake at 400 degrees 50-60 minutes. Cool. Serve with whipped cream.

Desserts

CARROT PUDDING

1 lb. carrots, sliced & cooked
1 c. milk
3 eggs
1/2 c. brown sugar
1 t cinnamon
1 t nutmeg
1/2 t ground cloves
1/8 t salt

Puree carrots in blender with milk. Pour into bowl and beat in remaining ingredients. Pour into six 2/3-cup buttered custard cups. Place in shallow baking dish and add water 1" deep in dish. Bake at 350 degrees for 35-40 minutes. Pass the whipped cream.

CARROT BROWNIES

1/2 c. butter
1 1/2 c. brown sugar
2 eggs
2 c. flour
2 t baking powder
1/2 t salt
1/4 t cinnamon
2 c. grated carrots
1/2 c. chopped walnuts
Powdered sugar

Melt butter in saucepan. Add sugar and stir well. Remove from heat and beat in eggs. Beat in remaining ingredients, except nuts and powdered sugar. Pour into 9x13-inch greased pan. Bake at 350 degrees for 30-40 minutes. Cool. Sprinkle with sugar.

POTATO DOUGHNUTS

1 c. sugar
1 c. hot mashed potatoes
2 T butter
2 eggs, beaten
1 c. milk
2 t baking powder
Flour
Salad oil

Mix sugar with potatoes. Add butter and mix well. Add eggs, milk, baking powder and enough flour to thicken into roll and cut. Fry a few at a time in hot oil until golden on each side. Eat as is or sprinkle with cinnamon and sugar.

INDIAN PUDDING

1 c. yellow corn meal
1/2 c. black molasses
1/4 c. sugar
1/4 c. butter
1/4 t salt
1/4 t ginger
1/2 t cinnamon
1/4 t baking soda
2 eggs, beaten
1 1/2 qts. hot milk, divided

Mix all ingredients thoroughly with half the milk. Pour into greased casserole and bake at 450 degrees 30 minutes. Stir in remaining hot milk and bake at 200 degrees 5-7 hours. Serves 8.

SWEET POTATO PUDDING

2 1/2 c. sweet potatoes, grated
1 c. molasses
2 eggs
2 c. evaporated milk
1 T melted butter
1 t ginger
1/4 t allspice
1 T brown sugar
1/2 t cinnamon

Combine sweet potatoes, molasses, eggs, milk, butter, ginger and allspice. Pour into a greased baking dish and bake at 350 degrees about 45 minutes, sprinkling the brown sugar and cinnamon over the top 20 minutes before serving.

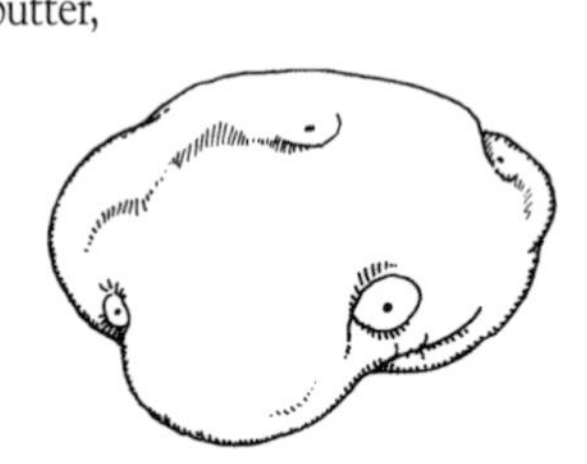

BUTTERMILK GLAZE

1/2 c. buttermilk
1 c. sugar
1/2 t baking soda
1 T white corn syrup

Beat all ingredients well. Pour over top of cake while still in pan. Let cake cool before removing from pan.

PUMPKIN CHIP COOKIES

2 c. pumpkin, cooked & mashed
2 t baking soda
4 t baking powder
1 t salt
2 t cinnamon
4 c. flour
2 c. sugar
2 eggs, beaten
1 T milk
1 c. salad oil
2 t vanilla
1 6-oz. pkg. chocolate chips
1 c. walnuts, chopped

Beat together all ingredients, except chocolate chips and walnuts. Stir in chocolate chips and walnuts. Drop by teaspoonfuls on greased cookie sheet. Bake at 375 degrees 12-14 minutes.

CARROT YOGURT SQUARES

2 c. whole wheat flour
1 c. white flour
2 t baking soda
1 t baking powder
1 t grated lemon peel
1 t salt

1 8-oz. carton lemon yogurt
3/4 c. honey
1/2 c. walnuts, chopped
2 eggs
1/2 c. salad oil
1/4 c. milk

Stir together flours, baking soda, baking powder, lemon peel and salt. In another bowl, mix other ingredients together. Add liquid all at once to dry ingredients, stirring only until flour is moistened. Spread in greased 9x13-inch pan. Bake at 350 degrees for 30-35 minutes. Cool and cut into squares. Makes 24.

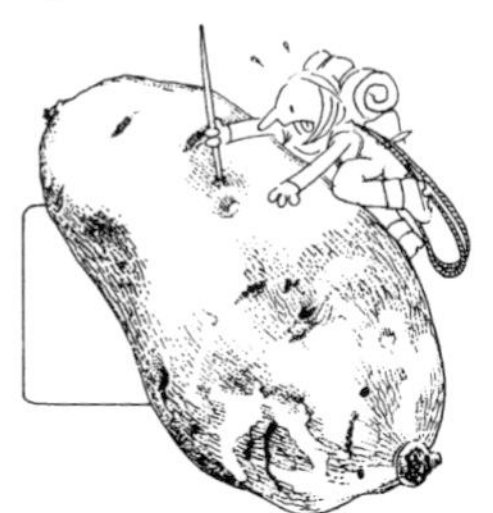

PUMPKIN CAKE

2 c. sugar
1 1/4 c. pumpkin, cooked & mashed
1 1/4 c. salad oil
4 eggs
3 c. flour
2 t baking powder
2 t cinnamon
1/2 t nutmeg
1/4 t cloves
1 t salt
1 c. raisins
1 c. walnuts, chopped

Combine sugar, pumpkin and oil. Beat in eggs. Sift dry ingredients and stir into batter. Fold in raisins and walnuts. Pour into a greased 10-inch tube pan. Bake at 350 degrees for 1 1/4 hours. Cool 10 minutes. Turn out onto serving dish. May be eaten as is or you can glaze with a thin mixture of powdered sugar and milk, if you wish.

PUMPKIN PIE SQUARES

1 c. flour
1/2 c. oats
1 c. brown sugar
1/2 c. butter
2 c. pumpkin, cooked and mashed
1 1/2 c. evaporated milk
2 eggs
3/4 c. sugar
1/2 t salt
1 t cinnamon
1/2 t ginger
1/4 t cloves
1/2 c. walnuts, chopped
2 T butter

Mix flour, oats and half the brown sugar. Cut in 1/2 c. butter until mixture is crumbly. Press into a 13 x 9-inch pan. Bake at 350 degrees for 15 minutes. Combine pumpkin, milk, eggs, sugar, salt and spices. Pour over baked crust and bake at 350 degrees for 20 minutes. Mix together nuts, 2 T butter and remaining brown sugar. Sprinkle over pumpkin filling. Bake 15-20 minutes longer. Cool and cut into 2-inch squares. Makes 24.

POTATO CAKE

1 c. butter
2 c. sugar
1 c. mashed potatoes
4 eggs, separated
2 c. flour
3 T cocoa
2 t baking powder
1 t cinnamon
1 t nutmeg
3/4 c. milk

Cream butter and sugar. Mix in potatoes and egg yolks. Sift dry ingredients and add to creamed mixture alternately with milk. Beat egg white until stiff. Fold into batter. Pour into three 9-inch greased cake pans. Bake at 350 degrees for 20 minutes, or until it passes the old toothpick in the center test. Frost

COUNTY FAIR CARROT CAKE

3 c. grated carrots
4 eggs
2 c. flour
1 1/2 c. salad oil
2 c. sugar
1 t baking powder
1 t salt
1 t vanilla
1 t cinnamon
1/4 t cloves
1 c. walnuts, chopped

Mix all ingredients together well. Pour into a 10-inch greased tube pan. Bake at 350 degrees for 1 1/2 hours. Remove from oven and glaze while still warm.

For a brochure describing other **eberly press** books, please write to:

eberly press

1004 Michigan Ave.

East Lansing, MI 48823